Storms, Sunshine, and Flowers

Fariece Dews Altice

By: Fariece Dews Altice

Created and Published by: City of Jabez, Jabez Publishing House,

Remnant Books

Designed by: City of Jabez

Copyright Disclaimer

U.S. Library of Congress Registration Catalog

Table of Contents

DEDICATION

"IN MY OWN WORDS"

This book is dedicated to my Lord and Savior Jesus Christ, in whom, I put my trust. To my wise and wonderful parents, who knew I could write before I did because they chose me to do all of their writing. To my fabulous girlfriend, Pauline Munson Chapman, who insisted that I write this book now because time is of the essence. "You have less time on this side than you have on the other side, she added." I thought she had a valid point, so I got busy and gathered my poems together. To my amazing daughter Mary "Mawiyah" Harrington, who critiques my poems, sometimes adding a little more flavor. Thank you, sweetheart, for your support and patience. I'm glad you never stopped listening and letting me read them to you. Thank you to all of my family and friends who have encouraged me to continue writing. To my wonderful church families: Multicultural Worship Center and Israel Baptist Church for your continued interest in my writing and offer of assistance. To my amazing bonus son, Leo Harrington III for introducing me to the publisher and insisting I go forward with my work. Special thank you to my intellectual and talented great grandson Malachi Gardner for inspiring me to come up with the title.

To my gifted and humble son, William Harrington who drew the picture of the rose on the cover of the book.

Most importantly, I'd like to thank my beautiful granddaughter, Asibi Carnegie for taking time out of her busy schedule to do everything possible to assist me with getting my book published; working with editing, design, and publishing team to bring my dream to reality. Without her vast knowledge and extremely skilled support, I would have been lost. A million hugs and kisses sweetheart. To everyone who gave me the push to get started, I shall be eternally grateful for you.

ACKNOWLEDGEMENT

I thank God who is first in my life by His grace and tender mercy. To my wonderful parents who raised all 16 of us to trust in God; to be humble, respecting ourselves and others, and to treat everyone the way we wish to be treated. I thank God for giving me the ability to write. Being from a large family taught me so many valuable lessons. Now that I have written a book of poetry – I'm compelled to write a book about my big, wonderful, and loving family. The way we laughed and joked with each other; we didn't expect much, didn't have much, but we had each other. To my oldest sister Vivian, who helped shape and mold my life. Even though she was tough at times, I loved her even more. To my debonair and caring brother Freddy, who was always at my side and never let me want for anything. To my brother Sam (the 9th child) who worked at a bakery as we younger ones couldn't wait for him to come home and bring us some eclairs – something we loved and never had before. Then he became an expert hunter and fisherman. He could catch three to four fish on his line before anyone else would catch one. His fishing and hunting skills helped my parents feed us. Thank you, Sam for your kindness and generosity. Love to my loving and attentive daughter Mary "Mawiyah" Harrington, who supported me and gave many great ideas and suggestions. To my dearly beloved children, William Harrington, Gwendolyn "Talibah" Harrington, LaVerne Llewellyn, and Barbara, who are all in Paradise awaiting my arrival. My nine grandchildren Anthony, Roger, Victor, Fariece, Asibi, LaKisha, Abdou, LaKenya and Carroll. 34 great grandchildren and eight great-great grandchildren – too numerous to name but not too many to love and adore. Thank God for my many blessings. I was able to give the kind of love one receives from a grandmother that unfortunately; I was not able to receive.

To the rest of my big and beautiful family – many nieces and nephews – the joy of my life. To my many cousins and sisters-in-law. My only living and loving brother, Wallace Henry Dews, I love you sweetheart for your caring and thoughtful ways.

I give thanks to my cousin Walter Robinson (Chicago, IL) whom I met for the first time Christmas 1975. He visited Washington, DC on a search to find his mother's sisters children; the most beautiful relationship I ever encountered. The following summer of 1976, my husband Everett got in his Eldorado with two of my brothers, John and Ferdinand "Freddy" and myself drove to Chicago, IL to meet Walter. The five of us then drove to Des Moines, Iowa where we met his brother

Edward and wife Barbara and children. We spent the week there and met cousins I'd never met before (Robinson's and Lowery's). While there, we made a pact that Walter would visit us every Christmas and we would visit him every summer and drive from Chicago to Des Moines. The first week we would stay at Barbara and Eddy's home. The second week, we'd stay at Walter's. Each year, my husband and I stayed at Barbara and Eddie's home. Their youngest daughter Diane always released her bedroom to my husband and me. Thank you, Diane. You are still doing nice things. Walter, a heartfelt thanks to you for making the first move. Rest in peace sweetheart. Those were the best 10 years of my life. We have since been able to stay in touch with our mid-west family, continuing to see one another on special occasions. Walter, we missed you at Barbara and Eddie's golden anniversary a few years ago. Since then they both have gone on to Paradise. I believe now you all are together again – loving each other like you always did.

To my long time and best girlfriend of over 50 years, Flora Greene; we share a friendship that includes both our families. To a loving lady Margaret Smith who befriend me and helped me care for my children when I moved into the Lincoln Heights project dwellings. To my childhood girlfriend Rachel Banks, whom I met when she was 14 and I was 12. Years would come and go but somehow our paths would cross, and we would be together again. Rachel, I miss you girl. All the activities you involved me in - I know you are in heaven somewhere encouraging someone to do something.

To my marvelous and wonderful late husband Clovice Altice, who loved to read my poems, who became so enthused that he suggested I enter writing contest from clippings he obtained from newspapers and magazines. After he passed away, I moved to Watertown, NY to be with my granddaughter, Asibi and my adorable great grandson Malachi. I later moved with her and her husband Courtney Carnegie to Pace, Florida where she and I joined a bowling league together. Three years later, I moved to Las Vegas with the help of another childhood friend, John Walter Johnson, my play brother who introduced me to some very nice friends. While there, I discovered I had family living on my father's side. I enjoyed four wonderful years in Las Vegas before returning home to be with my daughter Gwendolyn whom I lost two months later.

My journey has been blessed with so many wonderful people. Thanks to all of you. Some of my poems were created with a bit of humor in mind – hopefully to give someone a laugh or two. I firmly believe laughter is good for the soul and heals whatever ails you.

Fariece 'Baby" Dews

Being the 12th of 16 children, mother must have run out of names

Only "Baby" on my birth certificate is what it claims

When she took me home, she prayed for a name that would differ from the rest

She believed the name Fariece would suit me best

Then came the second name Opal which is a precious gem

She thanked God for the gift given to her from Him

I never knew vital statistics had no name on record for me

It wasn't until I applied for a passport you see

I must have been named Fariece before I started school

Because the record from school was the only tool

To confirm the name, Fariece was correct and true

Then my oldest brother got a notary and verified the statement too

I love the name Fariece, everyone tells me it's so beautiful and odd

Thank you, dear mother, for waiting on God

Full name of child _____ Bessy O ____

FATHER _____ MOTHER

2600 - 22nd Street, N. E.
Washington, D. C. 20018
May 18, 1981

To Whom It May Concern:

I, John Westley Dews, brother of Garnice Opal
Dews, verify that she was born to Ferdinand
William Dews and Mary Coles Dews on
November 30, 1931.

John W. Dews

3

DISTRICT OF COLUMBIA PUBLIC SCHOOLS | SCHOOL AUXILIARY SUPPORT SERVICES
Student Affairs Branch
825 North Capitol Street, N.E., 6th Floor
Washington, D.C. 20002
(202) 442-5110 • Fax (202) 442-5094

Date: September 10, 1999

Ms. Faricee Dews Jenkins

7324 Donnell Place,. C2

Forestville, MD 20747

Re: School Records Search Request

Dear Ms. Jenkins:

This is a response to your request for verification of personal data as shown on District of Columbia Public Schools records on file for the student listed below:

Birney Elementary School	September 1937
Name of School	Date of Record

NAME OF PUPIL: Farice Opal Dews

DATE OF BIRTH (OR AGE): November 30, 1931

PLACE OF BIRTH: Washington, D.C.

NAME OF FATHER: Fardinand W.

NAME OF MOTHER: Mary

NAME OF GUARDIAN:

REMARKS:

This verification is limited to the content of the student records on file. No information can be added or deleted. Any erasure nullifies this document.

Sincerely,

Michon E. Peck
Director (Acting)
Student Affairs

MEP/lm

4

Jesus Is Walking

Jesus is walking throughout this land

Giving us messages, we can understand

He's showing us signs all along the way

Promised He'd come, didn't name the day

He's walking. He's walking like a natural man

Jesus is walking throughout this land

We see wars and wars with different faces

Tsunami and hurricanes in divers' places

While the winds and the rains bring about the flood

We need to be on our knees pleading the blood

He's walking. He's walking bringing his band

Jesus is walking throughout this land

When Noah's Ark landed, the entire earth was dry

God said the fire next time and put a rainbow in the Sky

Stop the shootings and killings, let love abide

Have faith in God 'cause you can't hide

He's walking. He's walking He's all around

Better be ready when the trumpet sound

He's giving us time to get it right

He's coming back like a thief in the night

Looking for a church without a spot or wrinkle

Don't hope on a star. It might not twinkle

We won't know the minute nor the hour

Wake up, everybody! He's got the power!

Genuine Love is Priceless

I'm from Washington, DC born and bred

Twelve Brothers, three sisters, had to share my bed

Lived down the hill across from the railroad track

Ain't ashamed of where I come from and don't have to look back

Had no running water, no indoor plumbing

Dirt poor and didn't know it just kept on humming

Mother Taught us to respect and love one another

We didn't have much, but we had each other

I can remember as sure as you're born

All eight of us had a nylon stocking on Christmas morn

Filled with an apple, an orange and a tangerine

A few mixed nuts and some hard candy wrapped between

We didn't even get a gift, not even a toy

Just seeing those stockings filled our hearts with joy

It's not having a lot of things that make you good

It's good when you treat others like you know you should

Daddy walked the floor all night to make sure we were nice and warm

He covered us with extra blankets or overcoats or anything on his arm

Thank God my parents taught us to treat everyone the same

No matter what they looked like or their given name

To find and see some good in everyone

Regardless of their background or where they came from

We didn't fight each other as siblings do

We let me be me and you be you

Whenever we saw each other, we were greeted with a big hug and a kiss

I can't thank God enough for giving me such a wonderful and loving family as this

The Seeds in My Garden

I named my children flowers because I was very blessed

I believed God let me plant the finest and the best

To put into my garden and watch the flowers grow

To nourish and cherish and blossom galore

When they were coming up, they called me the warden

Because I was so in awe of my beautiful garden

I knew the Flowers and the way they performed

They couldn't get around me I was always armed

My firstborn a son William was my gardenia

So kind and gentle, yet sturdy and strong

He protected the girls even when they were wrong

My oldest daughter Mary, my beautiful rose

Those petals were vibrant. The thorns were not exposed

My third child Gwendolyn was my morning glory

No matter what she did or what time she went to bed

She was the first one in the morning to raise her genius head

My baby girl Laverne was my little sweet petunia

She fluttered like a butterfly, free and filled with joy

Hung out with her male cousins like she was a boy

I had another flower that peeped up through the soil

Her stems were underdeveloped. She didn't stay long at all

I know she is in the sacred garden blooming up a storm

In the mist of the other Flowers, so peaceful and warm

Vivian, We Thank You

You were the oldest of sixteen and you ran the show

Whatever happened in the family you had to know?

Throughout the day your phone was ringing

Some news, somebody was bringing

You had no children of your own

The way you treated us little ones, no one would have

known

You knew all our friends and their families too

You always asked how are they, what do they do?

If we didn't know the answer or gave a negative reply

You'd say you children make me sick. You don't ask why

You never forgot to wish happy birthday to whoever had a birthday

And then would call to ask if we called that person on their special

day

You taught us to love and obey the law

You said whatever we did the big man saw

So, we listened to you and didn't corrupt

Cause we knew you would scold us with those

hurting words "Grow up, Grow up"

Vivian, Biboo, Rema we love you so much

We will always miss your love and tender touch

Every time the phone would ring

You used to tell us everything

But you didn't call to tell us you were leaving

We only guessed you didn't want us grieving

That's alright, baby, you must have been tired

You fought a good fight, you really tried

God took you home to get your rest

Your job is done, you gave it your best

Vanishing Youth

Youth is like a big balloon that goes up, up and away

One minute full of tears then giggles the rest of the day

Full of energy and a great big open heart

No cares no worries so cute and so smart

Dressing and tying your own little shoes

Knowing it all, giving everybody the blues

As time goes on their ideas and their dreams

Expanding as the days go by it seems

Youth can be the most important stage of one's life

The next step is adolescence guide it without strife

Enjoy every moment from beginning to the end

Cause one day you'll awaken and ask yourself when

When did I leave my childhood for adolescence and then?

To become a grown-up person seemingly in a few hours

And face a whole new life in this great big world of ours

Now comes the time to decide which road I must take

Since my youth has vanished the decision is mine to make

It only seemed like yesterday. I thought I could fly

My oh my, how quickly the time went by

Love is the key

Love is the key to living

Love is the key to giving

If we love each other consistently

Like God loves you and me

Instead of pain and misery

There would be, love and peace and harmony

Love is a kind word or deed

Love is to help someone in need

Love is caring and worketh no ill

Whenever you learn to do God's will

He'll give you joy unspeakable joy

Like the kind He gave his baby boy

If your love of God is understood

Then love your neighbor like you know you should

Give God the praise, both night and day

Ask him to forgive you and show you the way

Love harbors no evil or animosity

Love is the key to generosity

Jesus died on the cross just for us

He never grumbled or even made a fuss

He gave His life so we may live

So, tell me what you must give

You can give him love. Love is free

He gave us a gift that will last until eternity

Top Model Pattern

Take: *Reesie's Voluptuous boobies*

Asibi's Coca-Cola waistline

Kisha's Plump Rump

Kenya's Gorgeous Long Legs

Then add: *Reesie's Beautiful thick locks*

Asibi's Pretty face and fabulous lashes

Kisha's Big bright, flashy eyes

Kenya's Cute little sunken dimples

Once this pattern is skillfully
woven together and given a whirl

It will be guaranteed to out rate
any Top Model, on any runway,
anywhere in the entire world

My Sister, My Friend

What can I write about Liz?

What can I say about Liz?

Except that she has always been the same way

Since the first time I met her to this very day

From the time she met Dewsie as she fondly

calls him

She's been like a jewel to the family a treasure,

a gem

When brother Clarence took this sweet young

girl to become his wife

It was the very beginning of a beautiful life

Together they had three handsome guys

Clarence, James, and William to fulfill their

lives

Clarence and Liz's door is always open to

family and friends

No ifs or buts or it depends

You are welcome, come in, come on sit down

Put your feet under the table and gather

around

Have some tea or coffee or something to eat

Every 4th of July they gave you a treat

The yard is full of guest. The grills are burning,

while Catherine and Virginia is sitting quietly by

Liz is greeting everyone, saying hello, hi

Always wearing a smile and would sometimes tease

With those big pretty eyes, I'd say now

child, please

Now, Liz, I know you wouldn't want me to

expose this folly

I just couldn't pass up the chance to get my jolly

Once, we visited Clarence and Trudy in N.C.

Liz kidded and teased the heck out of me

Well on our return trip, Liz asked me to do the driving

Sure, no problem I said all the time conniving

We drove for miles just chewing the fat

Then the devil told me don't let her get away with that

Suddenly, I pulled her car over and stopped in the grass

I said get out, get out, I'm going beat your

ask me no question. I'll tell you no lie

When I saw those big, beautiful Brown's, open

so wide... I laughed so hard I thought I'd die

Then we both laughed every now and then

While back on the road, heading for home again

Seriously Liz, all jokes aside you are the best,

you are the best sister-in-law anyone could want

You're my sister, my friend, my children's aunt

I thank God for placing you in our family

You added three branches to the Dews Oak Tree

We all love you and are proud to say

You brought a lot of happiness and blessings our way

My Beautiful Rose

Friday, July 15, 1949 70 years ago

A blossom developed and began to grow

When an explosion in the earth arose

Bringing ten tiny fingers and ten tiny toes

A smile so bright it lit up the earth

A million dollars couldn't equal it's worth

Those eyes were so piercing as they looked around

Wondering what about this place was so profound

Now that you've been here all this time

Have you found what makes the rhythm rhyme?

Or are you still inquisitive as you used to be

When you find what it is, will you please tell me

Teach Us Thy Way

Father, please bless us tonight

Guide us and teach us to do what is right

You are our creator Lord, you know all we do and say

From this moment on, please teach us to pray

Honoring your name in all we do

Living our lives in Remembrance of you

Give us an open mind and an open heart

To receive your message and never part

From a great book, we did nothing to earn

Please make us faithful and teach us to learn

About the gift you gave to everyone

Saving us from sin by sending your son

Amen

To My Childhood Friend

Until We Meet Again

Love you, Rachel, my dear and loving friend, for your tenacity, your kind of shyness your smile and your willingness to lend a helping hand.

Never in anybody's business but always able to handle your own.

Loved how you love to have a party and entertain those you cared for with plenty of food and surprises. You made everyone feel welcomed with your grace and charm.

I shall never forget that party of yours that I attended at your sister Dally's house, where she introduced me to pigs in a blanket. Remember. A piece of hot dog rolled up in a biscuit. I was 12 years old, and you were turning 14. Thanks for inviting me. That was my first party.

You were so much like your big sister, who loved to entertain and have friends around all the time.

Rachel, please let Dally know that the little Dews girl, your friend, never forgot her love and kindness.

And Rachel, one glorious day I will see you both, then I will thank her for myself. (smile) and please hug and kiss Marie for me.

PS,

I know Terry was your best friend, but she is my friend too

Love,

Fariece

Herbert Prindell White JR

He was released by the angels on September 17, 1951

Entered into this world as the number one son

Relaxed cool and calm sometimes a little shy

Bubba was the name most people knew him by

Every day he went to work was a hardworking man

Remembered his parents taught him to do the best you can

Three sisters, six brothers made up the White family clan

Philadelphia Eagles was his favorite football team

Redskins your home boys should have been it seem

If anyone confronted him or brought the subject up

Needless to open their mouth, he'd say they were corrupt

Dexter was the brother that was closest to him

Even though his buddy Hank was his very best friend

LaVerne was the lady he chose for his wife

Loving daughters Fariece and LaKisha completed his life

Western movies were his thing, gun smoke and rifleman

Having a soothing Peach Amsterdam with chips in his hand

In the backyard on Brooke Road family and friends met

They drank, talked trash, and good food was et

Everybody was together in any kind of weather

Just a plan and simple guy was his claim to fame

Remembered all the rules of winning at his game

A Mother's Love

A mother's love is a gift from heaven

A mother's love forgives 777 times seven

It's more precious than gold

A story untold

A mother's love is bigger than life

A mother's love knows no strife

Heals the pain

And reaches out again and again

A mother's love is warm and caring

Patient comforting teaching and sharing

A mother's love is unconditional

A measurement which is unattainable

A mother's love is encouragement and belief

Trusting in God be it joy or grief

Sometimes overseeing or pretending to be blind

Never doubting or unkind

A mother's love surpasses all understanding

Abiding while guiding never demanding

A mother's love isn't love of herself

But loving her loved ones despite themself

Apart in the War

My son is a soldier fighting in the war

In a land called Afghanistan away so far

I thought the war was ending and the troops

Were no longer needed there

The oath of bringing our loved one's home left me

in despair

I guess I don't understand the cause

But my son being a soldier first, wouldn't hesitate or pause

To put his life on the front line with the ultimate sacrifice

For serving a country he loves, there would be no thinking

twice

He serves and protects his country every day

And asks God to bless America, the beautiful USA

His bravery is so astounding

It keeps my heart a pounding

So, Lord after he serves his country with pride and dignity

I pray Dear Lord you send him home safely to his

loving family

Call on God

When you feel downhearted and all alone

Nothing in the world to call your own

Your family turned their backs on you

And you don't have a clue as to what to do

Call on God Call on God just call on God

When your so-called friends leave you in despair

Knowing you're lonely but they don't care

During the night

You can't see the light

Call on God Call on God just call on God

When you're old and grey

And don't know your way

Thinking that you're useless and don't feel well

Don't let that devil put you in hell

Call on God Call on God just call on God

Call him when you're up, Call him when you're down

Call him every time you turn around

Open your mouth. He'll hear your prayer

Call the name of God. He's everywhere

Call on God Call on God

Call on God Call on God

Call on God Just call on God

Rachel Ann Banks

Rachel was the kind of lady you could admire and adore

Absolutely nothing deterred her. She had energy galore

Computer class was the thing she looked forward to attend

Her interest let her classmates believe they too could comprehend

Everyone who met her knew they had a friend

Leaving a legacy on which her daughters and grandsons could defend

A wonderful mother, strong and proud

Never complained, never boisterous or loud

Natural beauty and instincts, those she endowed

Being a sports enthusiast, she tried and did it all

At tennis, ice skating, skiing, dancing or bowling, etc. she never had a fall

Nothing was out of reach for her. Her life was to inspire

Kindly letting everyone know "You can make it if you try"

Showing by example that no standards are ever too high

Destiny

When two hearts are destined to come together

Nothing on earth, not even stormy weather

Can alter the working of His mighty hand

While drafting for your life a master plan

You can be in the same town, cross

the same streets and never meet each other

Breathe the same air and smell the fragrance

of the same Flowers and never know each other

Feel the same rain fall from the sky and walk

in the same tracks of the glistening snow

and never touch each other

then many miles away from the same places you've

been and some of the same things you have seen

and done, a connection is made without either of you

having the slightest clue

When God in his infinite wisdom brings true love to you

He reveals someone you can trust if you trust in Him. When your

eyes meet, they will light up and even glow in the dark

Someone you can confide in, if you confide in Him, your smile will

be so bright as if touched by a spark

Someone you can love if you love Him, just the mere presence of

each other will make your hearts roar like thunder

What God puts together; no man can put asunder

Keep lifting Him and praising His name

In good times or bad times, sunshine or rain

Together you will share a lifetime of love, with joy

and happiness in all that you do

If you believe and have faith in the One who made

it all happens just for the two of you

Now if ever sometimes things get in your way

Always remember that God-given day

And look to your Heavenly Father above

For faith, for hope and especially love

He said the greatest of these three is love

I Corinthians 13:13

Until Then

My cousin, My friend, My brother

You portrayed a life, unlike any other

By being yourself with a million-dollar smile

Respect and truth were always your style

Only gentleness and love flowed from your heart

Together you and Freddy will make a new start

He spoke with a softness that few men possess

Everyone who met him was blessed

Raising his children and others too

Many will remember the kind things he would do

You might think of him as being very strong

Cause he fought the good fight, he lingered long

Oh God please keep him safely in your care

Unify him with Pat and his loved ones there

Some called him monk, other called him Stan

Inspiring us all a wonderful man

No, no. Oh no sweetheart, this is not the end

One sweet day we will see you again

Love

Your cousin, your friend, your sister

Fariece

I am who I am

Can I be someone that I'm not

Can they realize or have they forgot?

That I was created by your hand

And my life is guided by your command

I am that which I am you see

Making no changes just being me

Though tongues do wag and eyes portray

The senseless evils of today

Yet with my humble heart and mind

I asked for forgiveness so I could find

The peace to help and love them still

What your will, will be, shall be my will

Oh God I'll thank you all my days

For blessing me in so many ways

Because I know you are fair and just

And will change all things when you must

God made me who I am you see

That was the plan he had for me

Neither you nor I will ever understand

And will never know the Master's plan

I Love the Lord, Yes, I do

I love the Lord, yes, I do

I love the Lord. What about you?

He rested my body throughout the night

Woke me up to see the morning light

Put a song in my heart as the day rolled on

Promised never to forsake me or leave me alone

I love the Lord, yes, I do

I love the Lord. What about you?

When I was broke and didn't have a dime

He filled my Cup to the brim, right on time

Put food in my mouth and on my table

He's a mighty good God, I know he's able

Yes, he is, yes he is

I love the Lord, yes, I do

I love the Lord. What about you?

My heart was heavy, and my body was weak

He said I bless the strong and I bless the meek

Give it to me put it in my hands

Leave it and believe it, I'll make all the plans

I love the Lord, yes, I do

I love the Lord. What about you?

I love the Lord. I love the Lord

I love the Lord, yes, I do

Jesus Loves and Cares for Me

When I was a child, I was taught this song

And I would sing it all day long

Jesus loves me this I know

For the Bible tells me so

Little ones to him belong

They are weak, but He is strong

When I grew up, it made me cry

When I learned the reason why

Jesus died for me on Calvary's cross

Was crucified and paid the cost

To save my soul and cleanse my sin

That I might have life and live again

I now am old and know He cares

He watches over me and hears my prayers

When he says my child, you must come home

That old place you will no longer roam

I've prepared a place where you will be

Home on high with the Angels, My Father and Me

Then I'll say goodbye to those I love

And pray we'll meet again in heaven above

Listen My Children

Listen my children to what I say

Don't go to bed before you pray

You might be tired but do it anyway

The Lord, thy God, took care of you today

Mind your parents and your teachers too

Trust in God to tell you what to do

He'll grant you wisdom to see you through

The Lord, thy God, will take care of you

If you read your Bible regularly

Whether or not there's adversity

He'll give you life more abundantly

Cause God loves you unconditionally

Have faith in God and use your mind

Wear a smile and please be kind

All God's blessings you will find

The Lord, thy God, is so sublime

Always remember to give God the praise

Glorify him in all your ways

Lift him up. You'll see it pays

God will bless and keep you all your days

Freckles

I'm crazy about my little freckle face girl

She's the prettiest girl in the whole wide world

My girl got freckles all over her face

Them cute little dots are in the right place

Just love them freckles, them cute little freckles

She got them freckles from her head to her toes

How she got them ----- only God knows

If I could connect them from dot to dot

You can bet I wouldn't miss one damn spot

Just love them freckles, them cute little freckles

The more freckles she's got, the more I love

Wouldn't take nothing for my little lovey dove

When we walk through the mall or hold hands in the park

The thrill of her closeness gives me a spark

Oh boy them freckles, them cute little freckles

She dances in my dreams and lights up my night

I'd Lose my mind if she got out of my sight

Her freckles are like diamonds, more precious than gold

She's mine all mine to have and to hold

Just love them freckles, my little freckle face girl

She's the prettiest little girl in the whole wide world

Just love them freckles, them freckles, them freckles

Just love them freckles, them cute little freckles

Dad, Pop-Pop, Granddaddy, Unk

God gave you back the love you gave out

To them all you loved and cared so much about

You had a way with us children beyond measure

Your wisdom and kind deeds we will always treasure

You made us all feel special from time to time

But if we got out of line, you didn't mind

To let us know how you felt right on the spot

Never raising your voice but having it you were not

When we got on your last nerve, you just say "da hell"

And walk away like you meant it, but never did you yell

Whenever we needed advice, it was you we came to see

You sat right down and listened attentively

Regardless of the situation, you were always there

To do whatever necessary to let us know you care

We had the best that God could give "A One of a Kind Man"

If we had a problem, we knew you would understand

When you went and left us, you took the main link

And didn't look back to see if we would blink

We thank God we were blessed to have you here

One day we will see you when we get there

We know you are prancing around somewhere in glory

Waiting for us to come with good news about our story

With Love

Your children, grandchildren, nieces, and nephews

And all their friends when they heard the news

Mother Dear

Mother we love you, you are missed

Only God could give you to us to be kissed

Truly you have been everything and more

His wonderful gift we shall always adore

Eternally and forever mother, you were the best

Rest on sweetheart. You deserve the rest

Don't worry about us, mother. You told us not to cry

Even if all 16 don't get there today, we'll be there by and by

And when we come, we will all rejoice

Ranting and raving to hear your sweet voice

My Aunt Bessie "1946"

Listen Ollie, Listen Louise, Bessie, Stanley, and Lucille

What I'm telling you about your mom sure nough

is real

I remember at Christmas when I was just a little girl

She gave me the prettiest reindeer sweaters and socks in

the world

And oh my when she would come to visit us

How she and my daddy would make such a fuss

Dews, as she called him, would be talking their trash

It was hilarious. I tell you it was a bash

Aunt Bessie was a twin sister to my mother

Together they had 21 children. Aunt Bessie had 5

and her sister, my mother gave birth to the others

Which children belong to which one, you would

 never have known

Aunt Bessie treated us all like her very own

We were always happy to see Aunt Bessie's face

Cause we knew fun and laughter would surely

be in the place

Before she left, she would do a dance she

called the wobble

And show us how a turkey would scratch and gobble

I love to hear my mother tell us how Aunt Bessie

tricked their pa

She put a pair of his shoes on backward and laughed

ha ha

Because she had eaten all the strawberries, the

children began to cry

So, to replace the strawberries pa had picked, she went

into the patch and picked till it was dry

When their father discovered that the strawberry patch

had been raided, he did shout

I can see where the man went in, but I can't

see where he came out

Now listen, my Aunt Bessie was so stylish in her

red dress with sable wrapped around her back

Saying this is "1946" baby, I'm jitterbugging now

ain't Balling the Jack

Go ahead Aunt Bessie, keep strutting your stuff

Can't nobody tell me My Aunt Bessie ain't tough

Her favorite saying was "I'm loose as a bucket of juice"

If you ain't gonna dance, then turn me loose

Grancie, as she was affectionately called, was number

one in my book

Just to have her in my life was all it took

She was the real, the one and only Queen Bee

God loves you, Aunt Bessie, and so do we

Nature's Own Way

Did you ever see a scarlet tree, a brown or

Yellow one?

Have you ever seen the leaves transform

when autumn come?

Don't you ever wonder what happens to

the green

If you are a nature lover, then you must

know what I mean

For every season

Did you ever find the reason

Why things come alive in spring?

And all the birds sing

And in summer when everything is bright

And in winter when all is covered white

So in fall dormancy masters fall

How does it all happen or come about, can

you tell me

I have watched and wondered and it's

still a mystery

And if anyone should ask me, I'd

Reply by Jove!

That it could only be a miracle

from God above

The River Boat

Oh Riverboat, oh Riverboat whose wheels continually spin

You captured my heart the moment I walked in

As I heard Al Hibbler sing with his melodious voice

Made dining at the River Boat my one and only choice

Oh, how I loved its coziness, its decor and its style

Thoughts of the South came for my mind was

traveling by the mile

I knew I was in New York City with its crowded

streets and bright lights

But when I entered the River Boat, I envisioned

 other sights

I thought I saw Ole Miss. it passed up and down

I had the strangest feeling that it was river bound

And as I watched the wheel a turning

Somehow, I could not keep from yearning

That through a miracle the engine would start

Drifting away slowly, tearing me apart

Flourishing Flowers

The Flowers bloom in spring with precious tender blades

Beautiful colors and a multitude of shades

From a tiny seed rested deeply into the soil

With a watchful eye and careful toil

Comes cute little petals peeking out to say "how di do"

Some red, some purple, some yellow, some blue

Every color of the rainbow displays an amazing hue

Lilacs and roses and sunflowers so tall

Makes the summer season appear prettiest of all

Their sweet-scented fragrance flows throughout the air

And is inhaled from here to there and everywhere

They sometimes cause lovers to dine and spoon

Cause many things to happen in June

Now comes July while they are at their best

Ladies don't know how well they are blest

Don't let August catch you an old maid my dear

Your helpers the flowers will be leaving this year

They've been here sometime for two seasons have past

Finally, they too must recline at last

Fall has approached, they are dwindling out

The leaves begin scattering all about

Then comes winter with its cold, dry hours

Diminishing the life of our flourishing Flowers

My Cousin, My Brother

On Christmas Day Aunt Bessie was celebrating in

her merry way

Cheering everyone on as she would dance, sing and play

Oh, what a Christmas and a Christmas it was

The children went to bed early. You didn't hear a buzz

The next day found Aunt Bessie in the maternity ward

When Stanley was born, she said thank you, Lord

God had given her a bundle of joy

A big handsome and healthy baby boy

Though she loved her girls, she had three

Her son was a special addition to the family tree

Your charisma and smile made you stand out

With a charming demeanor, I'll always care about

Stanley, you will always be my number one

My mother's twin sister's only son

You were born my cousin, who was more like a brother

Neither love nor money would I trade for another

Lucille always said I loved you the best

Believe me, when I say, I can't tell you the rest

Honey, your youngest sister, envies our relationship

My fondest advice for her is just to zip her cute little lip

Gwendolyn D. Harrington

Gwendolyn, a Monday's child, born fair of face

Was loving and caring and full of grace

Everyone who met her loved her and her sense of humor

Never believed in gossiping or spreading a rumor

Dancing was her gift and that gift she did possess

On the dance floor, you can bet she was the best

Learning all she could was talented in so many ways

Young in spirit, firm in the faith, only listen to what she says

Nevertheless, a gem, a pleasure, a life lived, filled with praise

Delores, her given middle name she kept to my surprise

Having a great relationship with her children she desired

Asibi and Abdou gave her grandchildren she admired

Ranting and raving about the wonderful things they did

Remembering all the nice things to her, they said

Inspiring them to be whatever they wanted to be

Nothing in this world could keep them from being free

Gwendolyn was the first. It was her given name

Talibah was the name she chose, both one in the same

Only she knew why she changed her name. She was so very smart

Now be it Gwendolyn or Talibah, they both were a sweetheart

Love from Mama to:

"My beautiful Morning Glory"

God wanted you home sweetheart

To share your precious story

My Dear and Loving Friend

May 27th the year of 1916, God created a wonderful birth

An Angel descended from heaven to earth

Radiance showed all over her face

Giving and caring, she was full of grace

Asking never what was in it for her, just

Relying on God, whom she always put her trust

Every day her smile shown brighter and brighter

Through God's mercy, her burden became lighter

She's smiling at Helen, Johnnie, Don and Gloria saying

My place is in heaven now. There's no delaying

In our father's time, we will be together again

Trust him and praise him, our love will remain

He ascended me to heaven to be with my Pearl

The rest of my family and my darling son Earl

Margaret, we love you and didn't want you to go.

But God is the master. Only he runs the show.

Love Fariece

I'm the Best I Know

Hey look here Pete what's happening man
Nobody's seen you around lately
Say what's up bro it's been a long time
about a year and some to dately
Well I'm back in school upgrading my skills
Got me on a J-0-B and paying my bills
Got my thinking cap on and taking it slow
All about my business, I'm the best I know

I heard the greatest was Muhammad Ali
But he didn't have nothing on me
I'd rap all day and half the night
Talk about my old lady and you had a fight
Yea I'd look a partner straight in the eye and
stand up to him toe to toe
Because I know I'm the best I know

My best buddy went walking with his hoody on
He was shot, and now he's gone
I'll remember him as long as I live
And strive to give all that I can give

My whip ain't pimped out, but it's good to go
I'm moving now I'm the best I know

All the chicks they try to give me their money
I say take it back I don't want it, honey
Then they switch around in their designer clothes
Wearing long hair, 7-inch stilettos, painted nails and painted toes
Oh no, no, no that's no big show
Just look at me I'm the best I know

Now I'm into college and getting some knowledge
studying math and science and history
Just paying my dues to society
I will get married and have a lovely wife
And three little children to complete my life
I'm off the streets not hanging out anymore
I tell you, man, I'm the best I know

Getting it all together putting it all intact
Ain't gonna let nothing hold me back
I can do anything I put my mind to
Watch me now see what I do
I'm in it to win it there's no letting go
How you like me now, I'm the best I know

Is There Anybody Like My Lord

Is there anybody like my Lord

Anybody anybody

No, no, no, no, no

He was hung and beaten and crucified

Just for you and me, He died

Suffered to save us from our sin

So, we'd have life and live again

Is there anybody like my Lord

Anybody, anybody

No, no, no, no, no

He stills the waters and restores the soul

Prepares us for the streets of gold

Where the faithful feast on milk and honey

And every day is bright and sunny

Is there anybody like my Lord

Anybody, anybody

No, no, no, no, no

Look at what He did for you

Look at what He did for me

He's peace, joy, love and harmony

I wanna be with Him in eternity

Is there anybody like my Lord

Anybody anybody

No no, no no no

No no, no not one

No not one

To My daughter Mary Magdalene, oops! I Mean Mawiyah

Friday's child is loving and giving

You're all that and more by the life you're living

Your earth day was Friday, the 15th day of July

Holding you in my arms and singing a lullaby

Was all I could do when I saw your beautiful face

So perfectly formed by only God's tender grace

I watched you grow and take the world by storm

From Mary to Walter to Piggy to a courageous mom

Raising three wonderful sons was no easy task

But you did it all. You didn't even ask

How would I, how should I, how can I help them

To be strong black productive young men

My daughter, my love, I'm so proud to call you mine

Keep doing what you're doing. You're doing just fine

Keep smiling and dancing, but live a prayerful life

Baby give it your best, you needn't have strife

You were blessed with precious grandkids, teach them the way

God will give you the wisdom and strengthen you each day

Just like your stone the ruby, you are a precious gem

I thank God for you darling. I give all the praises to Him

Who from His promises have given you three score and ten

And because you love so freely, He'll bless you until the end

From your momma

With all my love